First Facts®

Expert Pet Care

CARING for Dogs

A 4D BOOK

by Tammy Gagne

Consultant:
Jennifer Zablotny, DVM
Member, American Veterinary Medical Association

D1511741

PEBBLE
a capstone imprint

Download the Capstone 4D™ app!

- Ask an adult to download the Capstone 4D app.

- Scan the cover and stars inside the book for additional content.

When you scan a spread, you'll find fun extra stuff to go with this book! You can also find these things on the web at www.capstone4D.com using the password: dogcare.27384

First Facts are published by Pebble
1710 Roe Crest Drive, North Mankato, Minnesota 56003
www.mycapstone.com

Copyright © 2019 by Pebble, a Capstone imprint. All rights reserved. No part of this publication may be reproduced in whole or in part, or stored in a retrieval system, or transmitted in any form or by any means, electronic, mechanical, photocopying, recording, or otherwise, without written permission of the publisher.

Library of Congress Cataloging-in-Publication Data
is available on the Library of Congress website.

ISBN 978-1-5435-2738-4 (library binding)
ISBN 978-1-5435-2744-5 (paperback)
ISBN 978-1-5435-2750-6 (ebook pdf)

Editorial Credits
Marissa Kirkman, editor; Sarah Bennett, designer; Tracy Cummins, media researcher; Laura Manthe, production specialist

Photo Credits
iStockphoto: kali9, 9, 10, tdub303, 15; Shutterstock: anetapics, 19, ANURAK PONGPATIMET, 6 (bed), ARTSILENSE, 24, Asia Images Group, 12, BIGANDT.COM, 21 Middle Right, Cynthia Valdez, 7, Darren Baker, 13, Dora Zett, 4, 21 Bottom, ekmelica, Design Element, Elayne Massaini, 21 Middle Left, Eric Isselee, Cover, Back Cover, 3, gpointstudio, 17, Grigorita Ko, 16, hd connelly, 6 (toys), Igor Normann, 18, maksimee, 6 (bowls), Martin Maun, 20, Moolkum, 6 (brush), Nicole Lienemann, 11, Okssi, 6 (leash), Roland IJdema, 21 Top, Susan Schmitz, 23, unguryanu, 5, vvvita, 8.

Printed in the United States of America.
PA017

Table of Contents

Your New Pet Dog

Are you looking for a pet to run and play with outside? A dog may be the perfect pet for you. Dogs and their owners can do many things together. Many dogs in need of homes are in **shelters**.

Smart dog owners prepare for the **responsibility**. There is much to learn before bringing your dog home.

FACT

There are many types of dogs. Your family will need to decide which type of dog is right for your home.

shelter—a place that takes care of lost or stray animals

responsibility—a duty or a job

Supplies You Will Need

Every dog needs bowls for food and water. Dogs should also have a few toys. Toys help keep them from chewing things they shouldn't.

Your dog will also need a bed, brush, and leash. Leashes attach to either a collar or a harness. ID tags and **microchips** can help if your dog is ever lost. They let people know who the dog's owner is.

microchip—a tiny device that stores information about an animal, such as its owner's name and address

FACT

Use a harness instead of
a collar with your dog to
teach leash manners. It is
easier to control a dog's
movement with a harness.

Bringing Your Pet Home

Your new dog may be tired or scared when you bring it home. Limit meetings to just your family for the first day. Use care as your dog meets other pets. Even friendly dogs can hurt cats or other small animals.

Start **housetraining** your dog right away. Puppies may have accidents until they learn where they should go to the bathroom.

FACT

Always introduce your dog to new people and animals slowly. Rushing can make your pet feel stressed.

housetrain—to teach a pet where to go to the bathroom

Food Gives Dogs Energy

Adult dogs should eat twice a day. Owners may feed them dry or wet food. Dry food is called kibble. Wet food usually comes in a can.

Puppies need special food made for their growing bodies. Because their stomachs are so small, they will need to eat three meals each day.

FACT

Dogs love getting treats. But too many treats can make a dog gain too much weight.

Cleaning Up

Dogs with long or thick hair need to be brushed and bathed often. Even shorthaired dogs that spend lots of time outside may also need more **grooming**.

It is important to clean up after your dog's **waste**. You should always take bags with you on a walk. Use them to scoop up the waste and throw it in the trash.

FACT

Never use your shampoo on your dog. Dogs need special shampoo that is made for them.

grooming—cleaning and making an animal look neat

waste—food that the body releases after it has been digested

Checkup Time

Even healthy dogs should visit a **veterinarian** once a year. Vets can give tips about feeding, grooming, and **training**. Sometimes dogs need to get shots from the doctor, just like people.

Your dog can be **spayed** or **neutered** when it is six months old. This keeps dogs from having puppies.

FACT

You can keep your dog calm at the vet by petting it gently. You can also bring a treat or two along.

veterinarian—a doctor trained to take care of animals

train—to prepare for something by learning and practicing new skills

spay—to operate on a female animal so it is unable to produce young

neuter—to operate on a male animal so it is unable to produce young

Life with a Dog

Just like you go to school to learn, your dog must learn too. You can teach your dog to "sit" and "stay." Some dogs even learn tricks like "roll over" and "fetch."

It is also important to give your dog plenty of playtime. Playing gives your pet exercise. This helps keep its body healthy. Games like fetch and hide-and-seek also exercise your pet's mind.

FACT

Your dog should always be the seeker when playing hide-and-seek. It helps teach your pet to come to you.

Your Dog Through the Years

Your dog will have more energy while it is young. Older dogs are calmer and like to sleep more.

Some dogs have longer **life spans** than others. Most dogs live at least 10 years. Some even live to be 15 or older. As an owner, make every day with your dog the best it can be.

life span—the number of years a certain kind of plant or animal usually lives

Dog Body Language

How a dog behaves tells people a lot about what it is feeling. Tail wagging often means a dog is happy. Growling is a sign the dog is angry. A dog that raises its nose into the air may sense another person or animal nearby.

FACT

Dogs bark for many reasons. They may be announcing a visitor, asking another animal to play, or simply saying hello.

Types of Dogs

Some of the most active dogs are:
- Golden Retrievers
- Labrador Retrievers
- Siberian Huskies

Labrador Retriever

Siberian Husky

Border Collie

German Shepherd

The smartest dogs include:
- Border Collies
- German Shepherds
- Poodles

21

Glossary

grooming (GROOM-ing)—cleaning and making an animal look neat

housetrain (HOUS-trayn)—to teach a pet where to go to the bathroom

life span (LIFE span)—the number of years a certain kind of plant or animal usually lives

microchip (MYE-kroh-chip)—a tiny device that stores information about an animal, such as its owner's name and address

neuter (NOO-tur)—to operate on a male animal so it is unable to produce young

responsibility (ri-spon-suh-BIL-uh-tee)—a duty or a job

shelter (SHEL-tur)—a place that takes care of lost or stray animals

spay (SPAY)—to operate on a female animal so it is unable to produce young

train (TRAYN)—to prepare for something by learning and practicing new skills

veterinarian (vet-ur-uh-NER-ee-uhn)—a doctor trained to take care of animals

waste (WAYST)—food that the body releases after it has been digested

Read More

Carney, Elizabeth. *Woof!: 100 Fun Facts About Dogs.* Fact Reader. Washington, D.C.: National Geographic, 2017.

Casteel, Seth. *It's a Puppy's Life.* Washington, D.C.: National Geographic Kids, 2018.

Gagne, Tammy. *The Dog Encyclopedia for Kids.* North Mankato, Minn.: Capstone Young Readers, 2017.

Internet Sites

Use FactHound to find Internet sites related to this book.

Visit *www.facthound.com*

Just type in 9781543527384 and go.

Super-cool stuff! Check out projects, games and lots more at **www.capstonekids.com**

Critical Thinking Questions

1. What kind of supplies will your dog need?

2. How often will your dog need to be washed, or groomed?

3. What kinds of games can you play with your dog?

Index